The Hebrew Alphabet
and
2001 to 2027

By

Kathryn Sitterle

Published by:

Amoq (Hebrew Roots)

www,ThePublishedWord.com

McDougal & Associates is an organization dedicated to the spreading of the Gospel of Jesus Christ to as many people as possible in the shortest time possible.

ISBN 978-1-964665-03-0 Trade Paper Edition

ISBN 978-1-964665-04-7 Case Laminate Edition

Printed on Demand in the U.S., the U.K, Australia and the UAE

Dedication

To the Alpha and Omega or Alef and Tav

Who is our Good Shepherd

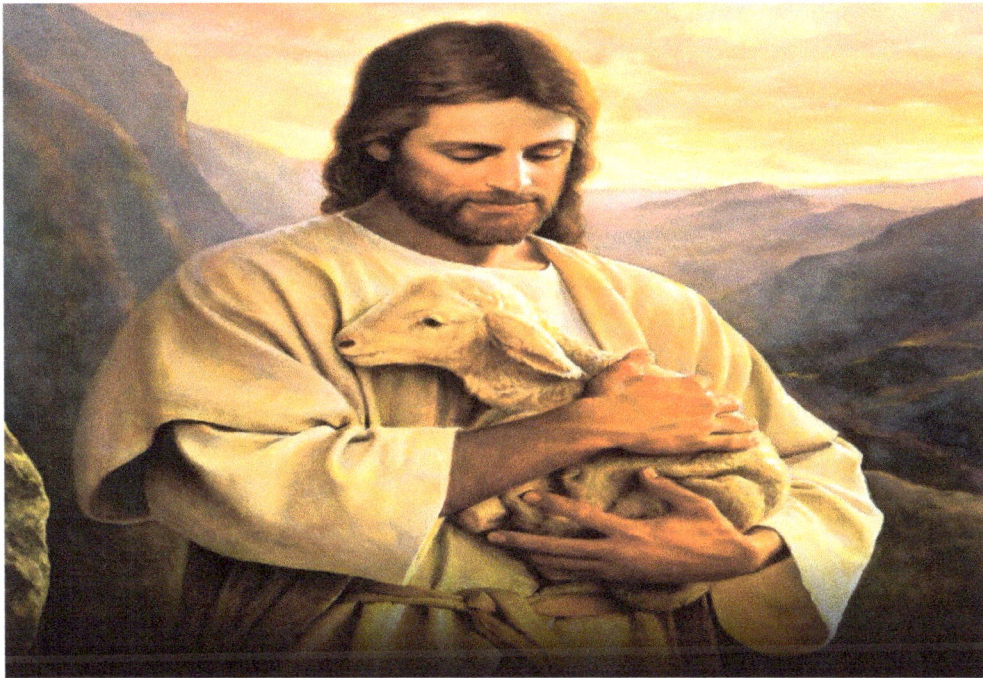

Without You, this, my first book, would not have been possible. You are my All, and I love You with all my heart.

THE AARONIC PRIESTLY BLESSING

(Numbers 6:24-27)

The LORD will bless you and He will keep you.

The LORD will make His face to shine upon you and He will be gracious to you.

The LORD will lift His countenance to you and He will establish Shalom for you.

And they will put My name upon the children of Israel and I will bless them.

CONTENTS

Introduction

But just as it has been Written:

"What eye did not see and ear did not hear and did not go up upon the heart of man, what God prepared for those who love Him."

But God has revealed them to us through the Spirit: for the Spirit searches all things, even the deep things of God.

1 Corinthians 2:9-10

Ever since I was fourteen years old, I have sought to know God and His truth. In 2010, I had a desire to learn the deeper things of the Lord, and shortly after that, the Lord had me study His Word and learn mysteries revealed there. Rabbi Jonathan Cahn's books, CDs, and DVDs have influenced me tremendously, especially *The Harbinger*,[1] which was released in 2011 and revealed patterns in ancient Israel that led to its fall from God's grace and how the U.S. appears to be following the same patterns of destruction.

My online church pastor, Steven Brooks, prophesied over me around the year 2012 that I was to write a book. A few months later I learned the book was going to be about how the years from 2001 to 2022 and beyond correspond to the Hebrew alphabet, which is comprised of 22 letters. This prophecy was given to me while my husband George and I and our two children, Katie and Andrew, were on our way to a vacation in Hilton Head Island in South Carolina. We had stopped in North Carolina to attend a Friday night church gathering that Pastor Brooks was holding in his church in Moravian Falls, before going on to our final destination the next day. Since that time, I have learned that the five final letters in the Hebrew alphabet also have an influence on the years 2012 to 2027.

Kathryn Sitterle

The Pictorial Hebrew Alphabet and the 21st Century

Is there an influence from the Hebrew alphabet on our 21 Century? Since ancient times, the Hebrew people, who lived in the Land of Canaan in the Middle East, known today as the nation of Israel or the Holy Land, have had an alphabet (Alef-Bet) system in which they could form words to communicate with one another. What is unique about this system is that their alphabet is pictorial, each letter having a corresponding picture. These pictures have evolved over the centuries but are fairly standardized today.

In this book, I will be using mostly the current pictures and their meanings as taken from Dr. Frank Seekins' book, *Hebrew Word Pictures*.[2] The pictures and their meanings appear to have a correlation to events that have occurred in this new century, starting with the year 2001 and going through to the year 2022 and beyond. As I have mentioned, there are 22 letters in the Hebrew alphabet, and five of them have a final form which extends their influence to the year 2027.

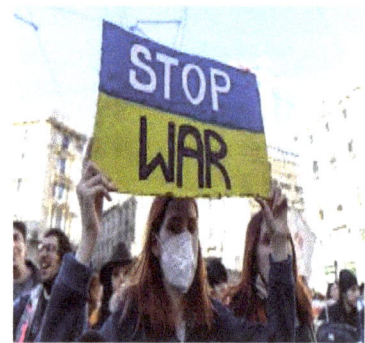

The Hebrew Alphabet and Pictographic Meanings

On the next few pages, I use some of the most commonly used names of the 22 letters of the Hebrew alphabet and pictures to show their influence for the first 22 years of this new century and beyond.

1 Alef　　　　**Ox**

2 Bet　　　　**House**

3 Gimel　　　　**Camel**

4 Dalet   **Door**

5 Hey   **Behold**

6 Vav   **Nail**

7 Zayin   **Weapon**

8 Chet   **Fence**

9 Tet   **Snake**

10 Yood   **Closed Hand**

11 Kaf   **Palm (Open)**

12 Lamed   **Staff**

13 Mem   **Water**

14 Noon   **Fish**

15 Samech   **Prop up**

16 Ayin   **Eye**

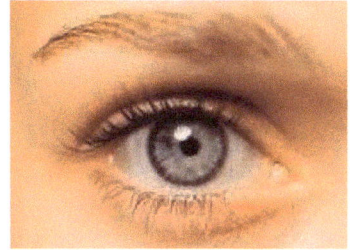

17 Pey   **Mouth**

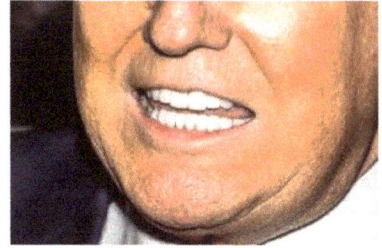

18 Tsadik   **Fishhook**

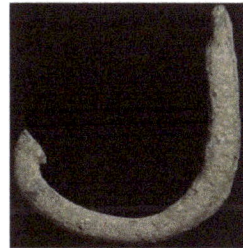

19 Koof   **Back Head**

20 Reysh   **Bowed Head**

21 Sheen   Teeth (Consume)

22 Tav   Sign (Covenant)

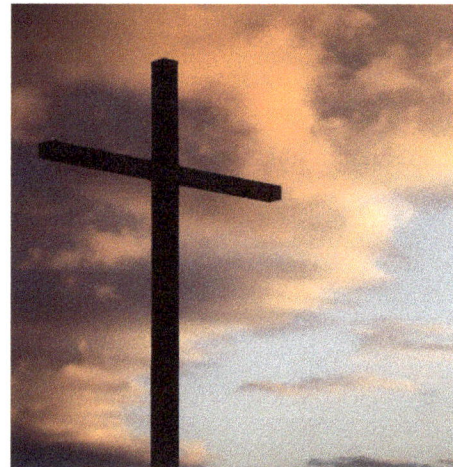

2001/5761-62 Hebrew Year

1 Alef   Picture: *Ox, Bull*

Woodland Musk Ox

Action: ***Burden Carrier with*** **Strength**

Numeric Value is 1 and Comment on the Alef in 2001:

Beginning, Unity and No other numbers are in the Alef

The definition of ox : Any cattle over four years of age that has been trained to do work.

Event Corresponding to the Alef (1) in 2001:

The September 11th attacks in New York City on the World Trade Center by the Islamic group Al-Qaeda prompted our nation to put in place new strategies to keep us safe. The U.S. and the world has an ongoing burden to this day to keep us all safe. Below is a picture of the clean-up needed to remove the destruction caused by the collapse of the World Trade Center and the burden of a widow having to start a new life.

2002/5762-63 Hebrew Year

2 Bet

Picture: House/Tent

Action: *Home, Family, Dwelling*

Numeric Value is 2 and Comment on the Bet in 2002:

Faithful Witness, Multiplication/Division, Agreement, Separation, Difference, Union

Event Corresponding to the Bet (2) in 2002:

This is continued from New York's Twin Towers Attack on 9/11 to households in America

More than 400,000 survivors, first responders, rescue and recovery workers, cleaning crews, lower Manhattan residents, and others are estimated to have been exposed to harmful toxins on 9/11 or during the nine-month rescue and recovery operations at Ground Zero. Tens of thousands nationwide are now suffering from chronic illnesses, including respiratory diseases, mental health issues, and more than 100 different types of cancer. More than 2,000 of those exposed have died.

The effect on many households of New York's Twin Towers Attack on September 11, 2001 continued well into 2002 and beyond.

Before the attack

During the attack

After the attack

The *New Yorker* online listed the number killed in the attacks as 2,753 and the number of New Yorkers suffering from post-traumatic stress disorder as 422,000. Many firefighters, police officers, and paramedics gave their lives in the aftermath of the attack trying to save others.

2003/5763-64 Hebrew Year

3 Gimel   **Picture: Camel**

Action: Lifted Up and Prideful

Numeric Value is 3 and Comment on the Gimel in 2003:

Godhead, Trinity, Resurrection, and Divine Completeness. Three is the symbol of the cube or solid contents. Therefore, it stands for that which is solid, real, substantial, complete, and entire.

Event Corresponding to the Gimel (3) in 2003:

Scientists with the World Health Organization found that MERS, a Covid-like virus, was active in camels in 2003 in the United Arab Emirates (UAE), 9 years before it was first found in humans. Writing in *Emergency Infectious Diseases from Germany and the UAE,* they reported that they had tested camel serum samples collected in 2003 and 2013 and found that most of them, including the 2003 specimens, contained antibodies to MERS.

2004/5764-65 Hebrew Year

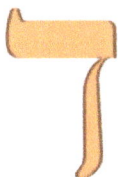

4 Dalet

Picture: Door

Action: To Enter, Pathway

Numeric Value is 4 and Comment on the Dalet in 2004:

God's Creative Works, Earthy, Four Directions (north, south, east, and west) and Four Seasons (spring, summer, fall, and winter) etc. Jesus/Yeshua is the Door that opens the way to Truth.

Events Corresponding to the Dalet (4) in 2004:

A door opened for same-sex marriage to become legalized in the United States, starting with Massachusetts on May 17, 2004.

August 9, 2004: A door to life on Mars and other planets opened as mankind's first-ever field geological study of another planet (Mars) began investigating the possibility of life on that planet.

Massachusetts legalized same-sex marriage on May 17, 2004.

The NASA Mars Rover arrives at a new site on the Martian surface.

2005/5765-66 Hebrew Year

5 Hey

Picture: **Behold**

Action: **To Show, To Reveal**

Numeric Value is 5 and Comment on the Hey in 2005:

Grace of God, Breath, Mystery of God, Redemption, Anointing, Favor.

Events Corresponding to the Hey (5) in 2005:

VATICAN CITY — Pope John Paul II died on April 2, 2005, breathing his last and ending a historic papacy of more than 26 years. His funeral brought together what was, at the time, the single largest gathering in history of heads of state outside the United Nations. Four kings, five queens, at least 70 presidents and prime ministers, and more than 14 leaders of other religions attended the funeral.

The body of Pope John Paul II

Behold: Your Messiah

Yitzhak Kaduri revealed the name of the Messiah as Yehoshua in Hebrew, Yeshua in Aramaic, and Jesus in English.

Yitzhak Kaduri was a Sephardic Jew who was born in Baghdad, Iraq, studied Kabbalah in his youth, and devoted his life to Torah study. By the fall of 2005 he was the most venerated rabbinical Jewish leader in Israel and proclaimed that he knew the name of the Jewish Messiah. He proclaimed the year 2005-2006 to be a year of "Secret and Revelation" and said that during that year the Jewish Messiah would be revealed. He left a note to his followers to be read a year after his death that would reveal the name of the Messiah. He died on January 28, 2006. A year after his death, the note he had written revealed the name of the Messiah to be Yehoshua (Joshua), or in English, Jesus.

February 15, 2005: YouTube, the popular Internet site on which videos may be shared and viewed by others, was launched in the United States.

2006/5766-67 Hebrew Year

6 Vav

Picture: Nail, Hook

Action: To Secure and To Add

Numeric value is 6 and Comment on the Vav in 2006:

Man. Man was created on the 6th day and has a carnal nature. There are 6 sides to an object. Physical completion, transformation, transition, and redemption are all characteristics of the number 6.

Events Corresponding to the Vav (6) in 2006:

Saddam Hussein was sentenced to death by hanging by an Iraqi court. Earlier in 2006 he had been charge by an Iraqi court for genocide against Iraq's population in 1988.

Saddam Hussein is hung

Construction of the One World Trade Center did not start until April 27, 2006

2007/5767-68 Hebrew Year

7 Zayin   **Picture: Weapon**

Action: To Cut Off, Cut

Numeric Value is 7 and Comment on the Zayin in 2007:

The Spirit of God, Completeness, Spiritual Perfection, Day of Rest, Finished, and Sacred.

Seven is considered the most sacred number to the Hebrews. It is found 735 times in the Bible. Some significant 7s:

7 Days the world was created	7 Trumpets in Revelation
7 Feasts were given in the Torah	7 Seals in Revelation
7 Branched Menorah	7 Bowls of Wrath in Revelation
7 Feasts given in the Torah	7 Churches in Revelation
7 Years to build Solomon's Temple	7 Stars
7 Years of plenty and 7 years of famine	7 Spirits

Event Corresponding to the Zayin (7) in 2007:

As President George W. Bush the 43rd entered the later years of his presidency, some Rabbis said that the number 43 signified an end. On the Day of Atonement, the High Priest would sprinkle the blood for a sin offering 43 times on the Mercy Seat. Some suggested that President Bush's presidency would be the end of the type of U.S. presidents we had had in the past. This would also line up with the number 7 as completion.

2008/5768-69 Hebrew Year

8 Chet

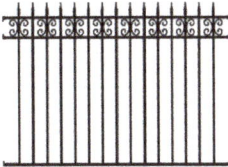

Picture: Fence, Inner Room

Action: A New Beginning, To Separate

Numeric Value is 8 and Comment on the Chet in 2008:

New Beginning(s), to Separate, Enclose. God's Salvation. A new beginning when God saved 8 people in Noah's day from the worldwide flood.

Event *Corresponding* to the Chet (8) in 2008:

November 4, 2008: Barack Obama became the first African-American to be elected President of the United States.

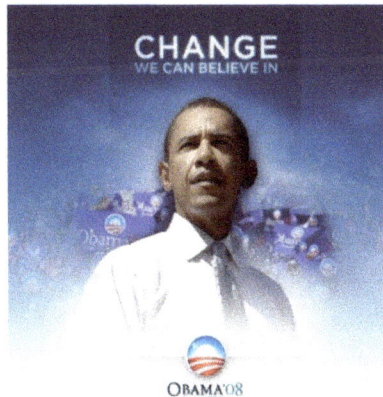

Popular end-time prophecy preachers claimed that Rabbis had stated that in the Torah it is decoded that the year 2008 would mark the beginning of the End of Times.

2009/5769-70 Hebrew Year

9 Tet

Picture: **Snake,**

Action: **To Surround**

Numeric Value is 9 and Comment on the Tet in 2009:

Fruit Bearing, Judgment, Enemy, Twisting of Truth, Finality of Single Numbers, Divine Completeness, Fruits and Gifts of the Holy Spirit (9), Birthing Babies usually takes 9 months.

Event Corresponding to the Tet (9) in 2009:

Mahmoud Ahmadinejad won the Iranian Presidential Election on June 12, 2009.

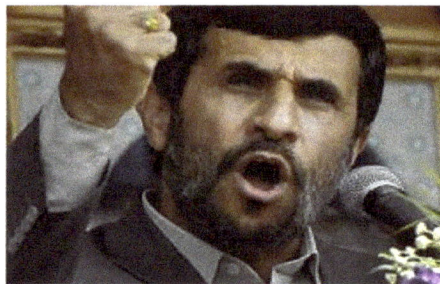

September 24, 2009: Prime Minister Benjamin Netanyahu of Israel addressed the United Nation General Assembly in New York stating that Iran posed a threat to the peace of the world, but Mahmoud Ahmadinejad repeatedly vowed: ***"Israel is to be destroyed and needs to be wiped off the map."***

2010/5770-71 Hebrew Year

10 Yood

Picture: **Hand (Closed)**

Action: **To Make, Work, A Deed**

Numeric Value is 10 and Comment on the Yood in 2010:

Perfect Order, Authority, Law and Responsibility, Dominion, Testing, Trials, the Tithe (10% to the Lord), Whole, Complete Development, Restoration, Perfection of Divine Order

Yood is the smallest Hebrew letter.

Events Corresponding to the Yood (10) in 2010:

On August 5, the San Jose gold and copper mine in northern Chile caved in while 33 miners were working underground, and the miners remained trapped underground for 69 days.

Closed: Miners stuck underground

To Make: Apple released the first iPad.

ד כ כ ך

11 Kaf/Chaf & Final Chaf

ך

The final Chaf:

Crowning Achievement

2012, Queen Elizabeth's

Diamond Jubilee

Picture: **Open Palm**

Action: **To Allow, To Open, To Cover**

Numeric Value is 20 and Comment on the Kaf in 2011:

Heroes Rising, Disorder, Confusion, Chaos, Incompleteness, Transition, the Number for Judgment.

Main Events Corresponding to the Open Kaf/Chaf (11) in 2011 (next page)

January 14, 2011: After weeks of violent protests in Tunisia that started with Mohamed Bouazizi, a fruit and vegetable seller who set himself on fire after police took his cart because he did not have a permit, President Zine El Abidine Ben Ali fled to Saudi Arabia, ending two decades of authoritarian rule in Tunisia.

January 25, 2011: Public dissent spread to Egypt.

February 2, 2011: Pro-government demonstrators and anti-government demonstrators clashed in Tahir Square in Cairo, Egypt.

February 3, 2011: Mass protests were seen in Yemen against President Ali Abdulla Saleh's three decades of rule.

February 11, 2011: Egyptian President Hosni Mubarak resigned due to protests against his rule.

February 14, 2011: Violence erupted in Bahrain.

February 15, 2011: Unrest developed in Libya.

March 16, 2011: The Syrians rose up against President Bashar Al Assad.

June 3, 2011: Yemen's president left the country.

October 20, 2011: Omar Gadhafi of Libya was killed by his own people.

November 28, 2011: Egyptians went to the polls, and the result was that the Muslim Brotherhood gained control of Egypt.

December 12, 2011: Syria's dead were estimated at 5,000.

Cairo, Egypt, Tahrir Square—February 2011

12   Lamed   **Picture: Staff, Cattle Goad**

Action: To Shepherd, Authority, Control

Numeric Value is 30 and Comment on the Lamed in 2012:

Lamed is a majestic letter that towers above all the other Hebrew letters from its position in the center of the Hebrew alphabet.

Governmental Perfection, God is in control and actively ruling as King. (The 12 Tribes of Israel and the 12 apostles). Apostolic Covenant flows through this number. Divine Organization, the Midnight Hour.

The name, Lamed is an acronym of *Lev Mevin Daat*, which is a *Heart that Understands Wisdom*. Just as the heart is the center of the human body, so the Lamed is in the center of the Hebrew Alphabet. Teaching, learning, and controlling the tongue are very important.

Main Event Corresponding to the Lamed (12) in 2012:

The Pope is the most recognized Shepherd of Christianity in the world.

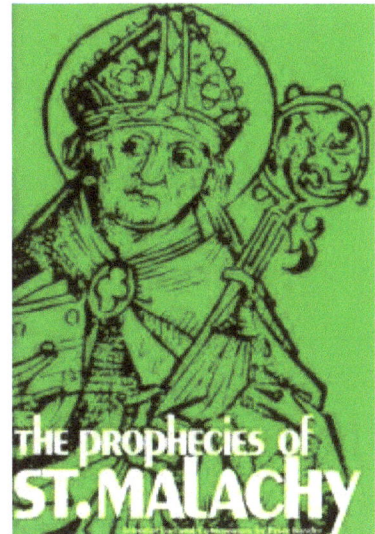

Pope Benedict resigned in 2012

Catholic St. Malachy's Prophecy of the Popes

The most famous and best-known prophecies about the popes are those attributed to St. Malachy. In 1139, he went to Rome to give an account of the affairs of his diocese to Pope Innocent II. He received a vision of the future, and before him was a long list of pontiffs who were to rule the Church until the end of time. There were to be 112 more popes after the pope of his day. The best-selling book, *Petrus Romanus: The Final Pope is Here*[3] by authors Tom Horn and Chris Putman uncovered many interesting facts concerning the popes of the 1900s to the present Pope Francis. Pope Francis is the 112th Pope (or the 113th Pope if you count the pope of St. Malachy's time period). St. Malachy wrote his prophecies in Latin because he believed the Latin speaking people would be in power at the end of the papal reign, that the pope would be an Italian, and that he would arrive on the scene in 2012. Even though Pope Francis did not become Pope until March 13, 2013, the Vatican newspaper published an article stating that Pope Benedict XVI had officially stepped down in the spring of 2012, fulfilling the prophecy that the last pope would come on the scene in the spring of 2012.

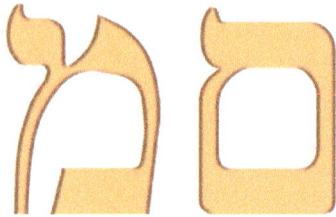

Mem and Mem Sofit

(Open Mem and Closed Mem)

Final Mem:

Conceal/Closed

(Will appear later in 2015)

A Concealed meeting in the White House

Picture: Massive Water

Action: Liquid, Chaos, Testing

Number Value is 40 and Comment on the Mem in 2013:

The Open Mem is associated with Revealing and can mean Deep Trouble.

The number 13 is associated with Rebellion, Apostacy, Rejection, and Backsliding.

Events Corresponding to the Open Mem (13) in 2013:

Edward Snowden, an American computer professional, leaked classified information from the National Security Agency (NSA) to the mainstream media starting in June 2013.

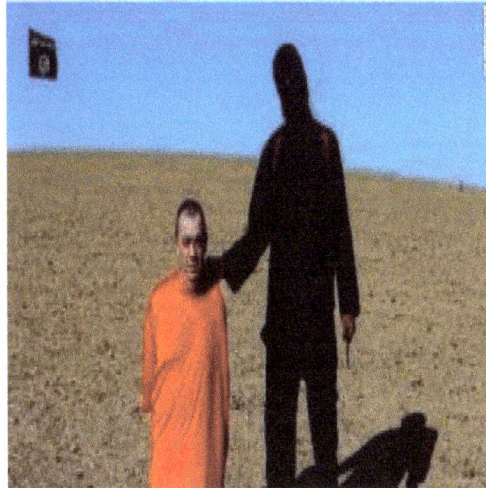

in 2013 the Federal Government opened the Utah Data Center (UDC), the country's largest spy center. *Watch what you say and do!*

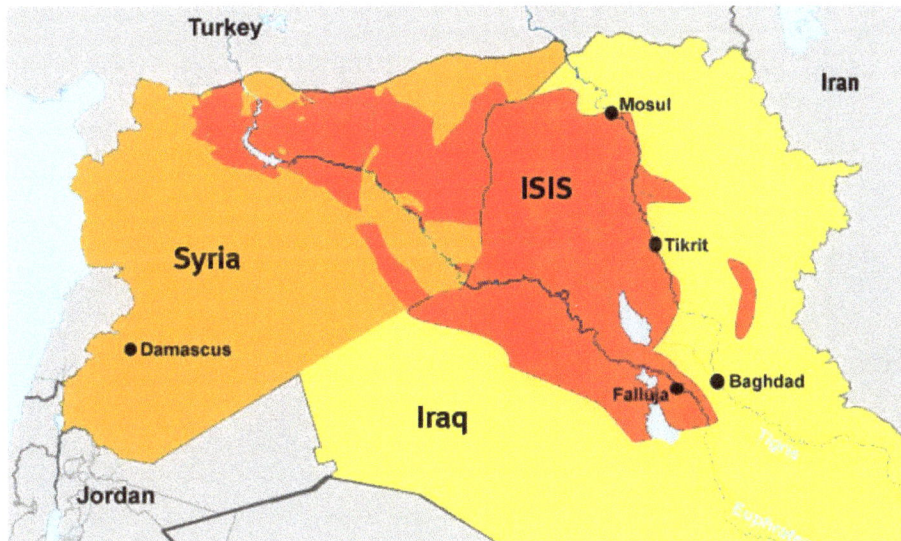

July 2013: ISIS began launching attacks almost every day against Iraqi citizens and security forces.

2014/5774-75 Hebrew Year

Noon & Final Noon

Final Noon:

Righteous Emerging

(Will appear later in 2017)

Righteous personalities

Picture: Fish Darting through Water

Action: Life and Activity

Number Value is 50 and Comment on the Noon in 2014:

Double Anointing, Generational Promises, Deliverance, Salvation, God's Faithfulness and Fear of the Lord.

Events Corresponding to the Fallen Noon (14) in 2014:

August 2014: In northern Iraq, only a quarter of the Assyrian population was left. Most of those not killed by ISIS had found refuge in neighboring countries.

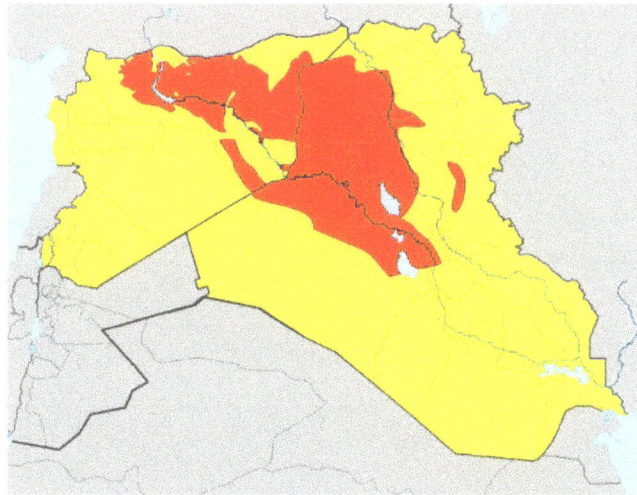

Christians being beheaded by ISIS

A Bent Noon can represent a Fallen State

(The fallen state of the U.S. in 2014)

1. **On** October 3, 2015, Russia overtook the United States in Nuclear Warhead Deployment as reported by the *Moscow Times.*

2. On May 26, 2015, China surpassed America as the largest economy in the world, as reported by *Value Walk,* an internet source.

2015/5775-76 Hebrew Year

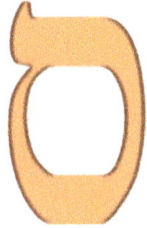

15 Samech   Picture: Prop

Action: Turn Slowly, Support, Twist

Number Value is 60 and Comment on the Samech in 2015:

Mercy, Rest, Acts brought about by Divine Grace, Divine Support, Enclosure, Closed Up, Divine Presence, Wedding Ring.

Events Corresponding to the Samech (15) in 2015:

September 20, 2011: It was reported that after the GAO (U.S. Government Accountability Office) audited the Federal Reserve, it had provided more than $16 trillion in total financial assistance to some of the largest financial institutions and corporations in the United States and throughout the world to prop up our way of life. Source: *Business Insider* 1/13/16. Bank of America, Citigroup, Morgan Stanley, JP Morgan Chases, and Wells Fargo were a few of the banks that were bailed out by our government. Some are pictured on the next page.

China's stock market crashed in 2015, dragging the U.S. and other stock markets lower. China spent $500 billion in 2015 to prop up the Yuan, *CNN Money* reported on January 7, 2016.

Saudi Arabia has been draining major assets by the billions to prop up their economy due to the drastic drop in oil prices as mentioned by Michael Snyder of *The EconomicCollapseBlog*.com.

16 Ayin   **Picture: Eye**

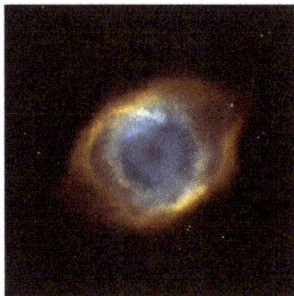

Action: To See, Know, or Experience

This picture, viewed from space, is said to be the eye of God. It has been visible since the 1800s but was made clearer by pictures from the Hubble Telescope in 2016, according to Wikipedia, the Online Dictionary

Number Value is 70 and Comment on the Ayin:

(Like the Aleph, Ayin has no sound of its own) *"Sweet 16"*

Events Corresponding to the Ayin (16) in 2016:

The people of Great Britain voted to leave the European Union.

The 2016 Presidential Election, November 8, 2016

Donald P. Trump, Republican Candidate for President of the United States, became the 45th President.

It was reported on a few television stations that for 2016 the Republican Platform was updated to follow more closely God's laws and principles. Therefore, Republican candidates for the presidency had to align their personal beliefs with that of the Republican Party.

2017/5776-77 Hebrew Year

Pey/Fey and Final Pey

Final Pey

Closed Mouth (Mask Wearing)

(Will appear later in 2020)

Picture: Mouth

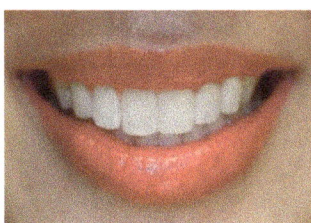

Action: Speak, Open the Mouth

Number Value is 80 and Comment on the Pey:

Overcoming to Complete Victory and Change or Transformation.

Events Corresponding to the Open Pey/Fey (17) in 2017:

January 20, 2017: Donald Trump was sworn in as the 45th President of the U.S.

December 2017: The U. S. officially recognized Jerusalem as the capital of Israel.

The city of Jerusalem's Western Wall and Temple Mount in gold

President Trump with Israeli Prime Minister Benjamin Netanyahu

2018/5778-79 Hebrew Year

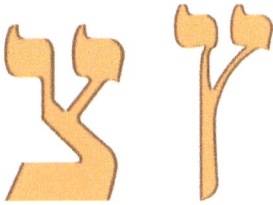

Tsadik and Tsadik Sofit

Final Tsadik

To Catch or Desire

(Will appear later in 2022)

Many are called home

Picture: Fishhook

Action: To Catch, Desire or Kneel in Prayer

Number Value is 90 and Comment on the Tsadik:

The number 18 has been associated with life more abundantly and the bondage of sin.

Event Corresponding to the Tsadik (18) in 2018

More people are going to Heaven now. Some, like my friend, Pastor James Durham of Higher Calling Ministries in Columbia, South Carolina, have been going daily. He wrote a book I have read about his heavenly visits entitled *What Heaven is Saying Today.*[4]

19 Koof

Picture: Back Head

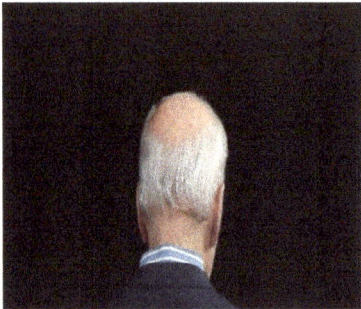

Action: The Last, Being Resurrected

Number Value is 100 and Comment on the Koof:

A number of the Lord, Ordering Judgment, and Faith is Important

Events Corresponding to the Koof (19) coming from behind in 2019:

Vice President Joe Biden, who was part of the last presidential administration, rose from behind in the polls against the then-current Trump Administration, to regain the Presidency for the Democratic Party.

October 27, 2019: Bernie Sanders told students to respect officers so they would not get shot "in the back of the head."

2020/5780-81 Hebrew Year

20 Reysh

Picture: Person the Head

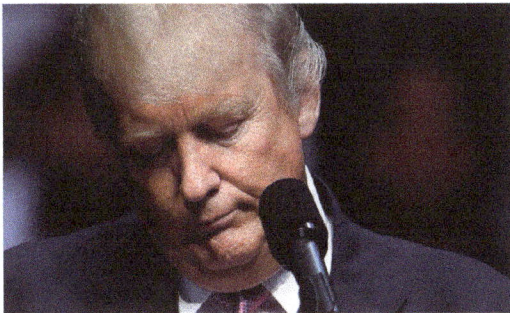

Action: The Head Person Humbled

Also, Wicked Happenings

Number Value is 200 and Comment on the Reysh:

The number associated with Prayer, Waiting and Expectancy for God to do something great.

Events Corresponding to the Reysh (20) in 2020:

President Trump was humbled by not winning a second term as president.

A year of anarchy in Portland and Seattle

The Coronavirus killed many

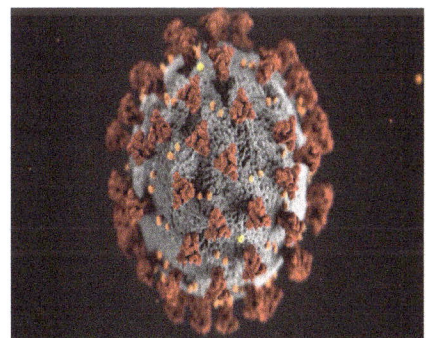

21 Sheen/Sin

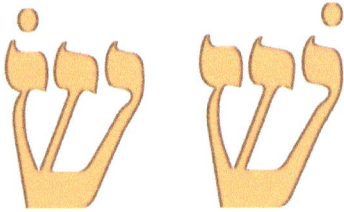

Picture: Teeth

Action: Consume or Destroy with the Teeth

Number Value is 300 and Comment on the Sheen/Sin:

When the Spirit (7) has perfectly completed His work, He displays things as they really are.

Events Corresponding to the Sheen (21) in 2021:

Be Brave and Follow your passions.

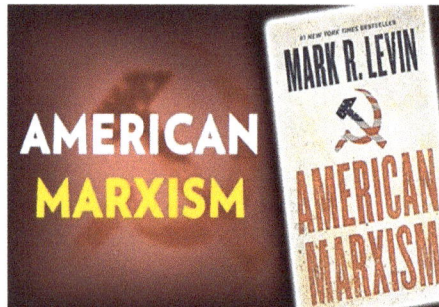

Russia moved tanks near the border with Ukraine, not only in Russia, but also in Belarus, preparing for a future invasion of that country.

Mark Levin wrote a book entitled, *American Marxism*,[5] describing how Marxism was currently devouring our United States of America.

2022/5782-83 Hebrew Year

22 Tav

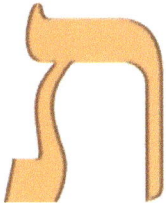

Picture: **Cross**

Action: To Seal or to Make a Covenant

Number Value is 400 and Comment on the Tav:

Divinely Perfect Period and Personal Revelation.

Event Corresponding to the Tav (22) in 2022:

The end of the Hebrew Alef-Bet is Tav and this year marked the end of Queen Elizabeth's reign over the United Kingdom and the other Commonwealth realms. (1952 to 2022).

These are the 5 Hebrew Letters that have a final form when they appear at the end of a word, and they sound the same as the letter they represent. We will see the influence they have in the Hebrew Aleph-Bet to the corresponding year they are associated with. The final letters:

1. **Final Chaf**   **Crowning Achievement**
   (11ᵗʰ letter)

   (Appears in 2012)

2. **Final Mem**   **Closed Door/Concealed**
   (13ᵗʰ letter)

   (Appears in 2014)

3. **Final Noon**   **Faithfulness/Dead Fish**
   (14ᵗʰ letter)

   (Appears in 2016)

4. **Final Fey**　　　　　　**To Close the Mouth**

　　(17th letter)　　　　　**Not to Speak**

　　(Appears in 2021)

5. **Final Tsade**　　　　　　**Being Upright**

　　(18th letter)　　　　　**The Righteous**

　　(Appears in 2023)

This book will go beyond the year 2022, and, by using the patterns in the Hebrew Alphabet, you will be able to continue to the year 2027.

Numbers that Preach[6] by Troy Brewer was used to give the meanings of numbers that seemed not to have much said about them regarding their apparent meaning in the Bible. It is an excellent resource that quotes many Bible scriptures that use numbers throughout both the Old and New Testaments.

2001 to 2022

The 22 Letters of the Hebrew Alphabet:

(Letters with the 5 Final Forms of the Hebrew are in red)

2001	Alef	Ox, Bull, Leader, King, Strength
2002	Bet/Vet	House, Tent, or Dwelling
2003	Gimel	Camel, Life Up in Pride
2004	Dalet	Door, Pathway, to Enter
2005	Hey	Behold, to Reveal
2006	Vav	Nail, Peg, to Secure
2007	Zayin	Weapon, to Cut, to Cut Off
2008	Chet	Fence, to Separate, Private, Inner Room
2009	Tet	Snake, to Surround
2010	Yood	Hand, to Make, Work, Closed Hand
2011	**Kaf/Chaf**	**Open Hand, to Allow, Chaos**
2012	Lamed	Shepherd's Staff, Authority, Control
2013	**Mem**	**Water, Massive, Chaos**
2014	**Noon**	**Fish, Activity, Faithfulness Emerging**
2015	Samech	Prop, to Slowly Turn, Support
2016	Ayin	Eye, to See, to Know or Experience
2017	**Pey/Fey**	**Mouth, to Speak, to Open**
2018	**Tsadik**	**Fishhook, Catch, Desire, or Need**
2019	Koof	Back of the Head, Behind, the Last, the Least
2020	Reysh	Bowed Head, a Person, the Head, Humble
2021	Sheen	Teeth, to Destroy or to Consume
2022	Tav	Sign, to Seal, to Covenant

2012 to 2027 and the Hebrew Alphabet's Influence

The 22 letters of the Hebrew alphabet with the 5 Final Forms added to extend out to the year 2027, starting with the Final Chaf, which is the 11th Hebrew letter and which affects the year 2012 ,and ending with the Final Tsade, the 18th letter in the Hebrew alphabet, ending with the year 2027

Letters with the 5 Final Forms will be shown in red.

2012   Final Kaf/Chaf (11) Final Form represents "Crowning Achievement." Queen Elizabeth's Diamond Jubilee was certainly a representation of her crowning achievements during her reign as Queen of Great Britain and the other Commonwealth nations.

2013   Lamed (12): Learning, Control and Authority

2014   Mem (13)" Water Revealed—Open Revealed

2015   Final Mem (13): Final Form represents Concealed or Closed

2016   Noon (14): Fallen State or it can represent Dead Fish

2017   Final Noon (14): Final Form can represent Righteous People Arising

2018   Samech (15): Support, Twist Slowly, Wedding Ring

2019   Ayin (16): Eye, Sight, Insight (Silence)

2020   Pey/Fey (17): Mouth, To Open (the Song of Solomon)

2021   Final Pey/Fey (17): Final form represents a Closed Mouth

2022   Tsadik (18): Fishhook Catch, a Desire or Need

2023   Tsadik (18): Sofit Final form represents Righteous Emerging

2024   Koof (19): Behind, the Last, the Least, Back of the Head, Resurrection, Mystery

2025   Reysh (20): Head, the ticked

2026   Sheen/Sin (21): Teeth, To Consume or Destroy

2027   Tav (22): Sign, To Seal, to Covenant

11th Letter, Final Chaf   **Crowning Achievement**

Crowning Achievement

In 2012 the world became aware of many of the *crowning achievements* of *Queen Elizabeth II,* who marked her 60th anniversary of being Britain's reigning monarch.

She was twenty-five when she became queen, holding true to the promises she made as princess. "I declare before you all that my whole life, whether it be long or short, shall be devoted to your service," she had said on her twenty-first birthday on April 21, 1947.

She has been just about everywhere and met just about everyone noteworthy.

She officially became the longest reigning British monarch on September 9, 2015.

She was one of the richest women in the world, but she was said to be a very thrifty person.

Elizabeth Alexandra Mary
Her Majesty The Queen

Queen's Diamond Jubilee
60 Years on The Throne

12th Letter, Lamed   **Shepherd's Staff, Authority**

Pope Francis

March 13, 2013: Jorge Bergoglio became the 266th Pope of the Catholic Church and the first to come from the Americas, having been a cardinal in Argentina.

13ᵗʰ Letter, Mem   **Open or Revealing**

Rabbi Jonathan Cahn is a Messianic Jewish author who became famous with his New York Times best-selling book, *The Harbinger[1]* in which he compares the United States and the September 11, 2001 attacks to ancient Israel and the destruction of the Kingdom of Israel. In his second New York Times best-selling book, *The Mystery of the Shemitah*, Rabbi Cahn discovered a seven-year pattern of the falling and rising of empires, the beginning of wars, stock market crashes, and the list of collapses, wars, economic woes, empires rising, etc.

Deuteronomy 15:1 *"At the end of seven years you will make a release."*

(This release is called a **Shemitah** and results in a release from field labor and from debts. In Hebrew, **Shemitah** also means **"a *fall, shaking,* or a *collapse."***

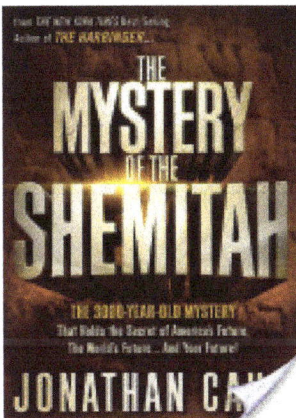

On Page 1, Jonathan Cahn, author of *The Mystery of the Shemitah,* asks the question: "Is it possible that there exists a 3000-year-old mystery that lies behind everything from the implosion of the New York Stock Exchange, the collapse of the American and world economy, the attack of 9/11, the rise of nations, the fall of nations, and events that have not yet happened but are yet to take place?"[7]

13th Letter, Final Mem   **Closed or Concealed**

February 14, 2015, U.S. President Barak Obama met with Muslim leaders in a closed-door meeting. The White House refused to reveal who all attended.

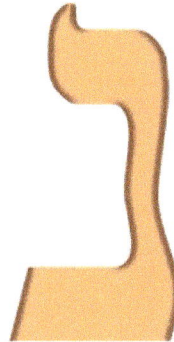

14th Letter, Noon   Fallen State

The 2016 U.S. Presidential Election was held on Tuesday, November 8, 2016. The Democratic ticket of former Secretary of State Hillary Clinton and U.S. Senator from Virginia Tim Kaine lost to the Republican ticket of businessman Donald Trump and Indiana Governor Mike Pence in what was considered one of the greatest upsets in American political history.

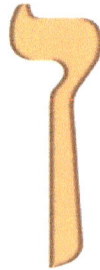

14th Letter, Final Noon   Upright People Arising

Billy Graham, one of the most upright American evangelists, urged Americans to vote for politicians who hold biblical values. He died on February 21, 2018. Two candidates who were seen as upright and who held biblical views emerged on the political scene in the United States from 2017 and beyond, to have a positive influence in our country and the world. They were Ted Cruz, U.S. Senator from Texas, and Ben Carson, who served as Secretary of Housing and Urban Development from 2017 to 2021.

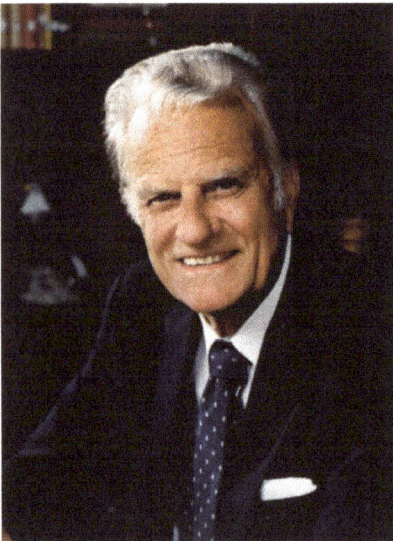

Reverand Billy Graham   **Senator Ted Cruz**   **Secretary of Housing Ben Carson**

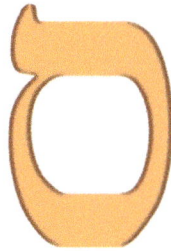

15th Letter, Samech   **Turn, Support, Twist**

Between 2017 and 2019, the Trump Administration cut nearly eight regulations for every new, significant regulation—more than fulfilling the promise of Executive Order 14771, to cut two regulations for every new regulation imposed.

The U.S. economy pepped up as a result of tax incentives and the removal of governmental regulations that had reduced business profitability for many businesses in the country. Unemployment, especially among teenagers and young adults, was at an all-time modern low, and many people were able to buy their first home.

16th Letter, Ayin   **To See, Experience and Gain Knowledge**

2019 was a year of protests. Hong Kong, Chile, Lebanon, Latin America, Indonesia, and India all had major protests that year.

Students in New York City protest for action to be taken on climate change.

The Amazon burns.

President Trump watched as Anthony Fauci, who oversaw research to prevent, diagnose, and treat infectious disease, immune-related illnesses, and allergies, addressed the American public with advice on the Covid Pandemic.

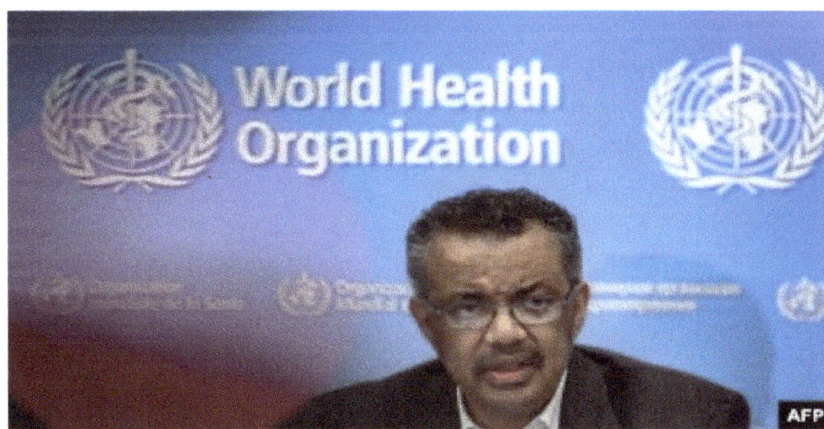

"Time is running out to stop the spread of Coronavirus," said the WHO in 2020.

17ᵗʰ Letter, Final Pey   **Closed Mouth**

The Omicron variant of Covid caused a new wave of concern for more Covid deaths and was cited as a reason to continue wearing a mask.

Covid cases, at first, were slow to show up in children, but started gaining in that age group in 2021.

18th Letter, Tsadik   **To Take Away or Catch up**

Marcus Lamb, President and Founder of DayStar Television, was reported to have died of Covid at the age of 64 on November 20, 2021 although it may have been due to a heart problem.

David Yonggi Cho also died.

David Yonggi Cho, the Korean Pentecostal who founded the world's largest megachurch, died on September 14, 2021 at the age of 85.

Queen Elizabeth was born April 21, 1926 and died on September 8, 2022.

She was Queen of England for seventy years, from 1952 to 2022, making her the longest reigning monarch in British history.

18th Letter, Final Tsadik   **Righteous People Rising Up**

Congressman Mike Johnson from Louisiana was elected 56th Speaker of the House of Representatives on October 25, 2023. He had spent his career fighting for the fundamental freedoms and traditional values that made our country the greatest in the world.

Ron DeSantis, the 46th Governor of Florida since 2019, ran for President of the United States on the Republican ticket.

In June of 2022, DeSantis decided against ordering Covid-19 vaccines for children under the age of 5, making Florida the only state to do so. He also stood against employers hiring or firing based on Covid-19 vaccines.

19th Letter, Koof   **The Last, Behind, Being Resurrected**

There would be a continuation of Koof's influence from 2021, when the Democrats took back control of the Presidency from the Republicans, who had taken it back from the Democrats from 2016 to 2020. In 2024, there is the possibility of the opposition having the same effect as what took place in 2016 and 2020.

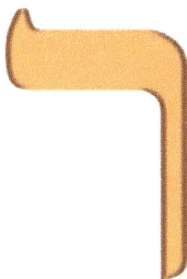

Reysh   **The Head Person and The Wicked**

This will be how President Donald Trump will deal with the wicked who challenge him and his administration

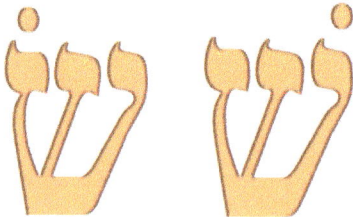

Shin/Sin   שׁ שׁ   To Consume or Destroy

Something or some things will be destroyed and/or consumed

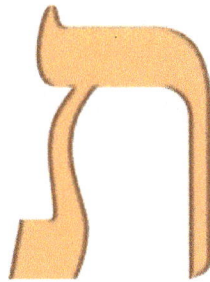

Tav   To Seal or To Covenant

To seal, make a covenant or a lasting agreement

Endnotes

1. Lake Mary, Florida (Frontline: 2012)

2. Olalla, Washington (Hebrew World Publishing: 2016)

3. Crane, Missouri (Defender Publishing: 2012)

4. Shippensburg, Pennsylvania (Destiny Image: 2020)

5. New York, New York (Threshold Editions: 2021)

6. Shippensburg, Pennsylvania (Destiny Image: 2024)

7. Lake Mary, Florida (Frontline: 2018)